![DK] **Watch me grow**

Bear

LONDON, NEW YORK, MUNICH,
MELBOURNE and DELHI

Written and edited by Lisa Magloff
Designed by Sonia Whillock,
Mary Sandberg, and Pilar Morales

Publishing Manager Sue Leonard
Managing Art Editor Clare Shedden
Jacket Design Simon Oon
Picture Researcher Marie Osborn
Production Shivani Pandey
DTP Designer Almudena Díaz

First published in Great Britain in 2003 by
Dorling Kindersley Limited
80 Strand, London WC2R 0RL

A Penguin Company

A CIP catalogue record for this book
is available from the British Library.

ISBN 1-4053-0241-0

Colour reproduction by
Media Development and Printing, Ltd.
Printed and bound by
South China Printing Co, Ltd., China

see our complete
catalogue at

www.dk.com

Contents

Come follow us and see how we GROW!

I'm a bear

I am the largest animal in the woods and forests where I live. I can swim and climb trees. My thick fur keeps me warm in winter.

I am king of the forest.

Peering around

Bears are curious. They often stand up on their back legs to look over the bushes.

Bears have long, sharp teeth and strong jaws.

The bear's sharp claws help it to hunt for food.

Turn the page and watch me grow.

Dad fights for mum

Dad had to fight with other male bears to see who would get to mate with mum. Dad was the biggest bear, so he won.

Grrr Grrrrr

The younger and smaller bear will lose the fight.

Their fight may look scary, but these bears are not trying to hurt each other. They are wrestling to see who is the strongest.

6

Go away! I am the strongest.

When the cubs are born
The mum and dad only stay
together for one or two weeks.
Then dad will leave and mum
will raise the cubs on her own.

Gripping facts

· ·

🐻 Mum and dad mate in
June or July, but their cubs
won't be born until the
next January.

🐻 Each bear has its own
area, called a territory.

🐻 Female bears can start
having cubs when they are
about four or five years old.

I'm born in the den

It's winter when we are born, but mum has found a warm, snug place to protect us from the cold and snow. The place where we live is called our den.

Bald and blind
This week-old cub was born tiny, blind and almost completely bald. It depends on its mother for everything.

During the cold winter, the mother bear does not eat. She spends all her time feeding her cubs, keeping them warm, and sleeping.

After one month, our eyes are open and we have fur.

I'm taking my first steps

After two months in the den, the weather is warmer and it's time for us to start exploring the world. We are ready to start learning all about how to be bears.

Watch and learn

Bear cubs are curious. They learn by watching mum and by playing.

My white collar makes it easy for mum to find me.

Milk from mum
Bear cubs get most of
their food by drinking milk
from their mother.

11

A walk in the woods

We are three months old and very good at walking. It's time for mum to teach us about the different foods we can find in the woods. We stay close to mum so she can protect us.

Berry nice
The young cubs feed on berries, insects and small animals such as frogs...yummy!

Wait for me, I'm right behind you!

The cubs have many new smells to learn about.

Mum is on the lookout for male bears who might hurt her cubs.

Bear-faced facts

🐻 Bears have a great sense of smell. They can smell food up to 2 km (1.2 m) away.

🐻 The cubs drink milk from mum until they are about five months old.

🐻 By watching mum carefully, the cubs learn what foods are safe to eat.

Mum on the lookout

Mum keeps watch for danger while we practise climbing trees. It's not as easy as it looks.

When she stands up, mum can see a long way away.

up we go...

...Whoops

Hold on tight!

Danger alert

A mother bear will chase off almost any danger. But hungry wolves are on the lookout for cubs that get separated from their mum.

Wolves

I'm learning to fish

It's time for me to join the older bears for my first fishing lesson. I learn how to catch the slippery fish by watching and copying the other bears.

This six-month-old cub is too small to stand in the fast-moving water, so he fishes from the shallow water at the edge.

The bears must wait patiently for the salmon to leap out of the water.

Clams for lunch

Bears love seafood of all kinds. This mother and cub are digging for clams. Their long claws are perfect clam openers.

Time for a long sleep

Winter is here, and there is not much food to eat. It's time to find a cosy place to go to sleep. We will sleep until spring, when there is more to eat.

These are my footprints.

The bears have grown fat during summer and autumn. The extra weight will nourish them until spring.

Bears grow a thick coat of winter fur.

These bears have dug
a snow cave to spend
the winter in.

I'm tired... time for bed.

The cubs
will share their
mother's den until
they are almost two.

19

The circle of life goes round and round

Now you know how I turned into a grown-up bear.

Here are my friends from around the world

The Sloth Bear lives in forests in India and Nepal. Its favourite food is termites.

The Giant Panda lives in China and eats only bamboo leaves and shoots.

I'm the world's biggest bear,

These American Black Bears live in forests and don't like open spaces.

My bear friends come in all sorts of different shapes and sizes.

Spectacled Bears are from South America. They build their nests in trees.

The smallest bear is the Asian Sun Bear.

and I live in the cold, snowy Arctic.

I'm a Black Bear cub.

Polar Bears' favourite foods are seals and walruses.

Friendly facts

Polar Bears are very good swimmers. They can swim for long distances without a rest.

A female bear is called a sow. A male bear is called a boar.

Bears see in colour and have much better hearing and smell than humans.

Glossary

Collar
The ring of white fur around the neck of all young cubs.

Nursing
When the mother bear feeds the cubs with her milk.

Sleeping
Bears usually sleep all winter. This is called hibernation.

Salmon
A type of fish that is very fatty. It is good food for bears.

Cub
For the first year of its life, a baby bear is called a cub.

Omnivore
An animal that eats almost anything. Bears are omnivores.

Acknowledgments
The publisher would like to thank the following for their kind permission to reproduce their images:
Position key: c=centre; b=bottom; l=left; r=right; t=top.
1: Lynn Rogers; 2-3: Nature Picture Library/Tom Mangelsen; 4: Still Pictures/Klein/Hubert; 5: Corbis/Greg Probst (r), /Michael T. Sedam (cl), /Steve Kaufman (bl); Oxford Scientific Films/Mathias Breiter (tl); Lynn Rogers (br); 6-7: ImageState/Pictor; 7: Michael S. Quinton (tr); 8: FLPA - Images of Nature/L. LeeRue (cl); 8-9: Lloyd Beebe; 10: Ardea London Ltd (cl main); 10: McDonald Wildlife Photography (cl, youngest cub); 10-11: McDonald Wildlife Photography; 11: Corbis/Kennan Ward (cr); 12: Nature Picture Library/Tom Mangelsen (l); 12-13: Nature Picture Library/ Steffan Widstrand; 14: Nature Picture Library/Steffan Widstrand (c); 14-15: McDonald Wildlife Photography (c), Getty Images/J.P. Fruchet (main); 15: McDonald Wildlife Photography (c, cr);
16: ImageState/Pictor (r), McDonald Wildlife Photography (bl); 17: ImageState/Pictor (tr, l), Lynn Rogers (cr); 18: Ardea London Ltd/Stefan Meyers (c), Corbis/Dan Guravich (tl), FLPA - Images of Nature/M. Newman (tr), Still Pictures/Francois Gilson (main); 19: Ardea London Ltd/Johan De Meester (b); 20: Corbis/Joe McDonald (cr below), Team Husar Wildlife Photography (tr), ImageState/Pictor (bc), FLPA - Images of Nature/ L. LeeRue (tc), McDonald Wildlife Photography (cr above), Lynn Rogers(tl, cl, bl, br), Andrew Rouse (c); 21: Corbis/Gunter Marx Photography (foreground); 22: Lynn Rogers (tl); 22-23: Oxford Scientific Films/Daniel Cox; 23: Oxford Scientific Films/Terry Heathcote (br); Lynn Rogers (cr); 24: Nature Picture Library/Tom Mangelsen (br), Lloyd Beebe (tr), ImageState/Pictor (cl), FLPA - Images of Nature/M. Hoshino/Minden (bl), McDonald Wildlife Photography (tl).
All other images copyright DK Images